SILLY

WACKY

CRAZY

FUNNY, TRUE

LAWS!!!

The Most Extensive Collection

by J.A. Lewis

Hundreds and hundreds and hundreds of laws, rules, and regulations that will make you laugh.

Copyright

To Squeak.

For getting your way,

Without saying a word

...and for making your own rules.

Preface

RULE 635

It's a crime to unlock your smartphone in the United States.

Are you thinking the same thing I am (whaaaaat)? I stumbled across this, in a newspaper article, while trying to have my second coffee of the day:

BY DECREE OF THE LIBRARIAN OF CONGRESS

IT SHALL HENCEFORCE BE ORDERED THAT AMERICANS SHALL NOT UNLOCK THEIR OWN SMARTPHONES.

PENALTY: In some situations, first time offenders may be fined up to $500,000, imprisoned for five years, or both. For repeat offenders, the maximum penalty increases to a fine of $1,000,000, imprisonment for up to ten years, or both.

This caught my eye. Especially because I own a smartphone and 2013 wasn't that long ago.

I wanted to see if it was a typo (it is not). Curiosity got the better of me and I started wondering...just how many weird laws are there on the books? What I found was amazing!

There are laws from all over the world, about every topic imaginable: hair, rats, mannequins, dirty cars, smelly feet, false teeth and even Santa Claus.

Some will make you laugh out loud, others will make you shake your head. Some will make you secretly want to meet their creator.

Many of the laws I found were generously supplied by newspaper articles (like the smartphone one). From there, I usually go backwards and conduct some research. Research is time consuming and I, surprisingly, found references for many of them (ouch!) but not all.

In the end, I decided to publish them all. The true purpose of this book is to make you chuckle or smile. I laughed many times during the compilation of this book. If you do just once, I have accomplished what I set out to do.

There is one thought that continues to nag me. For these laws to even exist, at some point in time, someone somewhere TRULY believed that each and every one of them made sense and served a purpose.

P.S. I labelled them as RULES...because I wanted to! Hope you enjoy them as much as I do.

This page is intentionally left blank.

Table of Contents

Chapter 1 - Alcohol

RULE No.288

In Kentucky, legally, you are deemed sober...unless you "cannot hold onto the ground".

. . . .

RULE No.383

The entire *Encyclopedia Britannica* is banned in the state of Texas because it contains a formula for making beer at home.

. . . .

RULE No.165

In Alaska, You cannot get drunk in a bar and remain on the premises.

. . . .

RULE No.319

Anyone under the age of 21, who takes out household rubbish containing even a single empty alcoholic drink container, can be charged with illegal possession of alcohol in the state of Missouri.

. . . .

RULE No.320

Drunkenness is deemed an "inalienable right", in the state of Missouri.

. . . .

RULE No.357

In Oklahoma, it's illegal to get fish drunk.

. . . .

RULE No.897

In the state of Washington, destroying someone else's beer cask or bottle is illegal.

. . . .

RULE No.712

In Louisiana, no one may pour a
drink, out on the ground, at any
drive-in movie.

. . . .

RULE No.885

In the state of Utah, alcohol may
not be sold, during an emergency.

. . . .

RULE No.325

In Nebraska, bar owners cannot sell
beer, unless they are simultaneously
brewing a kettle of soup.

. . . .

RULE No.333

In the town of Nyala, Nevada, you
are forbidden from buying drinks
for more than 3 people, other than
yourself, at any one period during
the day.

. . . .

RULE No.548

Plying a dog with alcohol is illegal,
in the state of Illinois.

. . . .

RULE No.170

In the state of Florida, owners of
commercial establishments, where
alcohol is sold, can be fined if they
participate or permit dwarf-tossing
contests.

. . . .

RULE No.173

In Indiana, liquor stores cannot sell
cooled water or soda. Uncooled
soda, however, is okay.

. . . .

RULE No.174

Liquor may not be sold by the
glass, in the state of Kansas.

. . . .

RULE No.800

It's illegal to sit on the curb of any city street and drink beer from a bucket, in the city of St. Louis, Missouri.

. . . .

RULE No.783

In Massachusetts, it's illegal to give beer to hospital patients.

. . . .

RULE No.784

In the state of Massachusetts, candy may not contain more than 1% alcohol.

. . . .

RULE No.796

In Columbia, Missouri, one may not drink in a bar between 2:00AM and 6:00AM.

. . . .

RULE No.767

In Athens-Clarke County, Georgia, it is illegal to sell two beers at once for a single price. For example, a bar cannot run a "2 beers for $5 special".

. . . .

RULE No.768

In the state of Hawaii, you may only have one alcoholic drink in front of you at a time.

. . . .

RULE No.157

In Switzerland, it is illegal to produce, store, sell and trade absinthe but it is legal to consume it.

. . . .

RULE No.573

In the state of Nevada, until the 1960s, it was illegal to sell alcohol at religious camp meetings, within 1/2 mile of the state prison, in the State Capitol Building, or to imbeciles.

. . . .

RULE No.601

In Pennsylvania, no man may purchase alcohol without written consent from his wife.

. . . .

RULE No.689

In the state of Illinois, it is illegal to give a dog whiskey.

. . . .

RULE No.271

In Indiana, it is against the law for any liquor store to sell milk.

. . . .

RULE No.660

In the state of Connecticut, you cannot buy any alcohol after 8PM, or on Sundays.

. . . .

RULE No.656

In Colorado, it is illegal to ride a horse while under the influence.

. . . .

RULE No.286

A person can be sent to jail for 5 years for merely sending a bottle of beer, wine or spirits as a gift to a friend in the state of Kentucky.

. . . .

RULE No.382

In Texas, you are not allowed to take more than 3 sips of beer at a time, while standing.

. . . .

Chapter 2 - Animals

RULE No.710

It's illegal to frighten a pigeon, in the state of Kentucky.

. . . .

RULE No.711

In Fort Thomas, Kentucky, dogs are prohibited to molest cars.

. . . .

RULE No.265

In Kirkland, Illinois, it is illegal for bees to fly over the village or through any of its streets.

. . . .

RULE No.13

In the state of Arkansas, alligators
may not be kept in bathtubs.

. . . .

RULE No.534

In Hawaii, owning a snake of any
kind is illegal, with the exception of
zoos, who are allowed to have two,
provided that they are both male
and non-venomous.

. . . .

RULE No.537

In the state of Idaho, anti-delinquency
statutes prohibit juveniles from
deliberately stepping on ants.

. . . .

RULE No.22

In Indiana, it is illegal to carry a dog
in your purse, if you have shoes on,
while walking across grass.

. . . .

RULE No.894

In the state of Washington, the harassing of Bigfoot, Sasquatch or other undiscovered subspecies is a felony, punishable by a fine and/or imprisonment.

. . . .

RULE No.874

The definition of "dumb animal" includes every living creature, in the state of Tennessee.

. . . .

RULE No.878

In Memphis, Tennessee, it's illegal for frogs to croak after 11PM.

. . . .

RULE No.72

In Israel, it is illegal to feed animals in public places.

. . . .

RULE No.73

In Israel, it is illegal to raise
Rotweilers.

. . . .

RULE No.829

In Barber, North Carolina, fights
between cats and dogs are prohibited.

. . . .

RULE No.53

In the state of Wyoming, it is
unlawful to own an albino monkey.

. . . .

RULE No.545

Monkeys were banned from smoking
cigarettes in South Bend, Indiana.

. . . .

RULE No.839

In the town of Bartlesville,
Oklahoma, no person may own
more than two adult cats.

. . . .

RULE No.834

In Canton, Ohio, if one loses their pet tiger, they must notify the authorities within one hour.

. . . .

RULE No.84

In France, no pig may be addressed as Napoleon by its owner.

. . . .

RULE No.314

Cats in International Falls, Minnesota are not allowed to chase dogs up telephone poles.

. . . .

RULE No.806

Worrying squirrels will not be tolerated, in the town of Excelsior Springs, Montana.

. . . .

RULE No.211

In Alaska, it is legal to shoot bears, but forbidden to wake a sleeping bear, for the purpose of taking a photograph of it.

. . . .

RULE No.778

In Waterboro, Maine, dog leashes may not be over 8 feet in length.

. . . .

RULE No.779

In Wells, Maine, deer may not be fed.

. . . .

RULE No.297

It is illegal to mistreat oysters, in the state of Maryland.

. . . .

RULE No.310

In Minnesota, it is against the law to tease skunks.

. . . .

RULE No.311

In the state of Minnesota, it is
illegal to cross the state line, with a
duck on your head.

. . . .

RULE No.759

In Belvedere, California, a City
Council order reads: "No dog shall
be in a public place without its
master on a leash."

. . . .

RULE No.736

In Billings, Montana, no person
shall raise pet rats.

. . . .

RULE No.513

In San Francisco, California, if
walking an elephant down Market
Street, it must be kept on a leash.

. . . .

RULE No.521

In Pine Ride, North Dakota, it is illegal for a dog to snarl in an unfriendly manner, at pizza delivery boys.

. . . .

RULE No.724

It is illegal to let your pig run free in Detroit, Michigan, unless it has a ring in its nose.

. . . .

RULE No.728

Citizens may not enter the state of Wisconsin with a chicken on their head.

. . . .

RULE No.606

In Monique Pass, Tennessee, it's a felony to allow a dog to eat a child's homework.

. . . .

RULE No.609

In Galveston, Texas, it is illegal to have a camel run loose in the street.

. . . .

RULE No.189

In the state of Wyoming, you cannot cut, sever, detach or mutilate more than ½ of a sheep's ear.

. . . .

RULE No.701

In Marshalltown, Iowa, horses are forbidden to eat fire hydrants.

. . . .

RULE No.237

In Hartford, Connecticut, it is unlawful to educate a dog.

. . . .

RULE No.253

It is illegal for a chicken to cross a road in Quitman, Georgia.

. . . .

RULE No.644

Dogs may not bark after 6PM in Little Rock, Arkansas.

. . . .

RULE No.636

In Mobile, Alabama, it is illegal for pigeons to eat pebbles from composite roofs.

. . . .

RULE No.256

It is unlawful for anyone to sleep in a dog kennel in Wallace, Idaho.

. . . .

RULE No.284

In Topeka, Kansas, it is against the law to annoy squirrels.

. . . .

RULE No.287

In Kentucky, you could be up on charges of contributory negligence for being behind a mule, without first speaking to the animal.

. . . .

RULE No.378

In Memphis, Tennessee, frogs are prohibited from croaking after 11pm.

. . . .

RULE No.379

In the state of Texas, it is illegal to put graffiti on someone else's cow.

. . . .

RULE No.654

In Colorado, the dog catcher must notify dogs of impounding, by posting for 3 consecutive days, a notice on a tree in the city park and along a public road running through said park.

. . . .

RULE No.416

You can't drag a dead horse down Yonge Street, Toronto, on a Sunday.

. . . .

RULE No.504

In Pacific Grove, California, it is a misdemeanor to kill a butterfly.

. . . .

RULE No.507

It's an offense to detain a homing pigeon, in the state of California.

. . . .

RULE No.592

It is illegal to make ugly faces at a dog, in Oklahoma.

. . . .

RULE No.617

In the state of Virginia, chickens must lay eggs between 8am and 4pm, not before or after.

Chapter 3 - Business

RULE No.913

In the state of Wyoming, junk dealers may not make any business transactions with drunk persons.

. . . .

RULE No.51

In Hoquiam, Virginia, it is illegal to tip a waiter more than 15% of the total bill.

. . . .

RULE No.341

In Newark, New Jersey, it is against the law to sell ice cream after 6pm, unless customers have notes from their doctors.

. . . .

RULE No.861

In Newtown, Pennsylvania, every outlet or switch that is installed (some of which can be purchased for $0.59) requires an electrical inspection fee of $1.33.

. . . .

RULE No.60

In the U.K., with the exception of carrots, most goods cannot be sold on Sunday.

. . . .

RULE No.66

Everyone in Finland must pay a TV tax, whether they own a TV or not.

. . . .

RULE No.67

In Finland, cab drivers who play music in their cars must pay royalties, for paying customers.

. . . .

RULE No.76

In Germany, every office must
have a view of the sky.

. . . .

RULE No.171

In the state of Hawaii, billboards
are banned.

. . . .

RULE No.100

A fee is levied on each purchaser of
any plastic bottle which is
returned. upon return of the bottle,
in Denmark.

. . . .

RULE No.113

Businesses must provide rails for
tying up horses, in Canada.

. . . .

RULE No.122

In Australia, Under the Australian
Communications Authority (ACA)
regulations, a modem cannot pick
up on the first ring.

. . . .

RULE No.764

The state of Florida (accidentally)
banned all computers and smart
phones in internet cafes.

. . . .

RULE No.133

In the Netherlands, prostitution is
legal but prostitutes must pay
taxes, like any other business.

. . . .

RULE No.136

In Norway, licenses must be
bought in order to own television
sets and VCRs.

. . . .

RULE No.756

In both San Jose and Sunnyvale, California, it is illegal for grocery stores to provide plastic bags.

. . . .

RULE No.574

In Las Vegas, Nevada, it is against the law to pawn your dentures.

. . . .

RULE No.576

In Willingsborough, New Jersey, it is illegal to display a "for sale" sign outside your house.

. . . .

RULE No.166

In Arizona, you cannot feed garbage to pigs without obtaining a permit first. This permit must also be renewed annually.

. . . .

RULE No.175

In the state of Maryland, a person who sells non-latex condoms, by means of a vending machine, is guilty of a misdemeanor and subject to fines.

. . . .

RULE No.511

In Los Angeles, California, babies are forbidden to ride alongside food, in supermarket trolleys.

. . . .

RULE No.519

In Connecticut, restaurant owners are required to provide separate nose blowing and non-nose blowing sections, in their restaurants.

. . . .

RULE No.595

In Grants Pass, Oregon, you can throw onions at obnoxious salesmen, if they won't stop knocking on your door or ringing your doorbell.

. . . .

RULE No.607

In the state of Tennessee, you are not allowed to sell hollow logs.

. . . .

RULE No.611

In Clarendon, Texas, lawyers must accept eggs, chickens or other produce (as well as money) as payment of legal fees.

. . . .

RULE No.719

In Maryland, it is a violation of city code to sell chicks or ducklings to a minor, within 1 week of the Easter holiday.

. . . .

RULE No.194

In Everett, Washington, it is illegal to display a hypnotized or allegedly hypnotized person in a store window.

. . . .

RULE No.435

A bill in 1976 ordered all business signs in the province of Quebec, Canada be written in French. Should the business operator wish to have English on the sign, the French wording should be at least double the size of the English word.

. . . .

RULE No.699

In the state of Indiana, it is illegal to sell cars on Sunday.

. . . .

RULE No.377

In Memphis, Tennessee
restaurants, it is prohibited to give
pie to fellow diners. It is also illegal
to take unfinished pie home.

. . . .

RULE No.385

In Houston, Texas, beer many not
be purchased after midnight on
Sunday, but can be purchased
anytime on Monday.

. . . .

RULE No.409

In the state of Wisconsin, cheese-
making requires a cheese maker's
license and Limburger cheese-
making requires a master cheese
maker's license.

. . . .

Chapter 4 - Death

RULE No.7

According to U.S. Federal Law, you
can be fined up to 1 million dollars
for partaking in the act of
Genocide.

. . . .

RULE No.911

In Sun Prairie, Wisconsin, cats are
forbidden from entering
cemeteries.

. . . .

RULE No.470

In Milan, Italy, people are legally
required to smile at all times.
There are exemptions for patients
in hospitals, or for those attending
funerals.

. . . .

RULE No.471

In Italy, it is illegal to make coffins out of anything other than wood or nutshells.

. . . .

RULE No.476

In Japan, It's illegal to wear the color purple unless you are mourning the dead.

. . . .

RULE No.870

In Spartanbur, South Carolina, eating watermelons in the Magnolia Street cemetery is forbidden.

. . . .

RULE No.496

In Turkey, all drivers must carry a hygienic body bag, suitable for transporting a corpse weighing up to 264lbs (120kilos), or face a fine and up to 6 months in jail.

. . . .

RULE No.865

In South Carolina, it's a capital
offense to inadvertently kill
someone while attempting suicide.

. . . .

RULE No.61

In the United Kingdom, suicide is a
capital crime, punishable by death.

. . . .

RULE No.557

In Massachusetts, mourners may
not eat more than 3 sandwiches at
a wake, after attending a funeral.

. . . .

RULE No.842

In Oklahoma City, Oklahoma, one
may not tip over a casket at a
funeral.

. . . .

RULE No.81

In France, you can legally marry a
dead person, as long as preliminary
civic formalities show that you and
your fiancé had planned to marry
before your fiancé died.

. . . .

RULE No.86

In France, it is forbidden to die, on
the territory of the commune,
without a cemetery plot.

. . . .

RULE No.315

It is still legal to kill your servant,
in the state of Mississippi.

. . . .

RULE No.98

There is a penalty of 20 krone
(USD3.00) for not reporting when
a person has died, in Denmark.

. . . .

RULE No.114

It's illegal to kill a sick person by frightening them, in Canada.

. . . .

RULE No.780

In Wells, Maine, advertisements may not be placed in cemeteries.

. . . .

RULE No.126

It is illegal to die in the Italian village of Falciano del Massico.

. . . .

RULE No.565

In Detroit, Michigan, it is illegal to loiter in the city morgue.

. . . .

RULE No.566

In the state of Minnesota, a tax form asks for your date of death.

. . . .

RULE No.526

In Florida, if you try to commit suicide and do not succeed, you are free. However, if you do succeed, it is a felony and you can be jailed.

. . . .

RULE No.466

There are more than 100 offenses that carry the death penalty, in Iran.

. . . .

RULE No.235

You risk a $5 fine by carrying a corpse in a taxi in Hartford, Connecticut.

. . . .

RULE No.674

In the state of Georgia, it is illegal to have a picnic in a graveyard.

. . . .

RULE No.672

In Georgia, it is illegal to use
profanity in front of a dead body
which lies in a funeral home or in a
coroner's office.

. . . .

RULE No.344

The penalty for jumping off a
building in the state of New York is
death.

. . . .

RULE No.614

Swearing in front of a dead person
is illegal, in the state of Utah.

. . . .

Chapter 5 - Driving

RULE No.1

In some U.S. states (e.g. Florida, California), a motorist can be cited for driving below the speed limit.

. . . .

RULE No.2

In the state of California, no vehicle without a driver may exceed 60 miles per hour.

. . . .

RULE No.541

In Illinois, it is legally stipulated that a car must be driven with the steering wheel.

. . . .

RULE No.23

In the state of Indiana, you cannot
ride a horse more than 10 miles
per hour, on any street in the city.

. . . .

RULE No.35

In New York City, you can receive
a $350 fine, if you honk your horn.

. . . .

RULE No.883

It's illegal to do "U-Turns", in
Richardson, Texas.

. . . .

RULE No.42

In Youngstown, Ohio, it is illegal to
run out of gas.

. . . .

RULE No.45

In Grants Pass, Oregon, it is illegal
to pump your own gas. You can
receive a ticket of $1,000.

. . . .

RULE No.485

In San Salvador, drunk drivers can
be punished by death before a
firing squad.

. . . .

RULE No.489

In Saudi Arabia, women are not
allowed to drive cars.

. . . .

RULE No.55

In the U.K., cows cannot be driven
down the roadway between 10am–
7pm, unless there is prior approval
from the Commissioner of Police.

. . . .

RULE No.558

It's illegal to shave while driving, in the state of Massachusetts.

. . . .

RULE No.838

In Oklahoma, tissues are not to be found in the back of one's car.

. . . .

RULE No.845

In the state of Oregon, drivers must yield to pedestrians who are standing on the sidewalk.

. . . .

RULE No.846

One may not test their physical endurance while driving a car on a highway, in Oregon.

. . . .

RULE No.847

In the state of Oregon, babies may not be carried on the running boards of a car.

. . . .

RULE No.68

In Zimbabwe, citizens may not make offensive gestures at passing motorcades.

. . . .

RULE No.70

In Israel, you cannot ride a bicycle without a license.

. . . .

RULE No.79

In Germany, it is illegal for your car to run out of gas on the Autobahn.

. . . .

RULE No.819

In New Jersey, if you have been convicted of driving while intoxicated, you may never again apply for personalized license plates.

. . . .

RULE No.88

In Denmark, before starting your car you are required to check lights, brakes, steering and honk your horn.

. . . .

RULE No.90

In Denmark, if your vehicle stalls and you leave it on the side of the road, you must mark the vehicle with a red, reflecting triangle.

. . . .

RULE No.92

In Denmark, if a horse drawn carriage
is trying to pass a car and the horse
becomes uneasy, the owner of the car
is required to pull over and if
necessary, cover the car.

. . . .

RULE No.94

In Denmark, no one may start a car while
someone is underneath the vehicle.

. . . .

RULE No.96

In Denmark, when driving, you must
have someone in front of your car
with a flag to warn horse drawn
carriages that a motorcar is coming.

. . . .

RULE No.323

In the small town of Whitehall,
Montana, it is against the law to
operate a vehicle with ice picks
attached to the wheels.

. . . .

RULE No.816

Before they do so, drivers must
warn those they pass on highways,
in the state of New Jersey.

. . . .

RULE No.102

Drivers of power-driven vehicles
who stop at pedestrian crossings
are liable to a fine of up to five
yuan (USD0.75), or a warning, in
China.

. . . .

RULE No.216

In Glendale, Arizona, it is illegal to
drive a car in reverse.

. . . .

RULE No.788

In Massachusetts, gorillas are not
allowed in the back seat of any car.

. . . .

RULE No.793

In Minnetonka, Minnesota, driving
a truck with dirty tires is
considered a public nuisance.

. . . .

RULE No.119

In Australia, you may never leave
your car keys in an unattended
vehicle.

. . . .

RULE No.130

In Mexico, bicycle riders may not
lift either foot from the pedals, as
it might result in a loss of control.

. . . .

RULE No.309

In the state of Minnesota, double-
parkers can be put on a chain
gang.

. . . .

RULE No.758

In Arcadia, California, peacocks have the right of way to cross any street, including driveways.

. . . .

RULE No.770

In the state of Illinois, it is illegal to hang obstructions from the rear view mirror, including fuzzy dice, air fresheners, GPS units, etc.

. . . .

RULE No.446

In Finland, the Helsinki Police do not issue parking tickets to motorists who illegally park; instead, they deflate their car tires.

. . . .

RULE No.449

In Finland, if you get fined for speeding or some other crime, the amount you are requested to pay to the courts relates to your personal financial position. The richer you are, the more you pay.

RULE No.452

In London, it is illegal to drive a car
without sitting in the front seat.

. . . .

RULE No.458

In Greece, a driver's license can be
revoked if the driver is
deemed poorly dressed or even
appears to be unwashed.

. . . .

RULE No.153

In Switzerland, you may not wash
your car on Sunday.

. . . .

RULE No.158

In Switzerland, every car with
snow tires has to have a sticker on
its dashboard. The sticker must tell
the driver that he should not drive
faster than 160 km/h (100 mph)
with these tires.

RULE No.159

In Switzerland, if you forget your car keys inside the car and leave the car open, you will be punished.

. . . .

RULE No.160

In the Philippines, cars with license plates that end with a 1 or 2 are not allowed on the roads on Monday. Those that end with a 3 or 4 are not allowed on Tuesdays. Those that end with a 5 or 6 are not allowed on Wednesday, 7 or 8 are not allowed on Thursdays, and 9 or 0 are not allowed on Fridays from 7am.

. . . .

RULE No.162

In Thailand, you must wear a shirt while driving a car.

. . . .

RULE No.579

In New Mexico, it is illegal for
women to pump gas. Instead, men
must willingly volunteer to pump
for single women. The same rule
applies to flat tires.

. . . .

RULE No.746

In the state of Alabama, you must
have windshield wipers on your
car.

. . . .

RULE No.729

In Minnesota, all men driving
motorcycles must wear shirts.

. . . .

RULE No.730

In Minneapolis, Minnesota, red cars
may not drive down Lake Street.

. . . .

RULE No.734

In the state of Missouri, it is not illegal to speed.

. . . .

RULE No.185

In Oregon, throwing urine or feces from a vehicle is illegal. Also, you cannot leave a container with those substances on the side of the road.

. . . .

RULE No.196

In Youngstown, Ohio, you may not run out of gas.

. . . .

RULE No.437

Although the speed limit in Ontario, Canada is 80kph (50 mph) for motorcars, cyclists have the right of way.

. . . .

RULE No.483

In Russia, it is illegal to drive a
dirty car.

. . . .

RULE No.688

In the state of Illinois, you must
contact the police before entering
the city in an automobile.

. . . .

RULE No.690

Cars may not be driven through
the town in Crete, Illinois.

. . . .

RULE No.702

In the state of Kansas, pedestrians
crossing the highways at night
must wear tail lights.

. . . .

RULE No.236

In New Britain, Connecticut, the speed limit for fire trucks is 25 mph, even when going to a fire.

. . . .

RULE No.662

In the state of Connecticut, it is illegal to discharge a firearm from a public highway.

. . . .

RULE No.640

In Anchorage, Alaska, it is illegal for a person to tie their pet dog to the roof of a car.

. . . .

RULE No.345

The state of New York has a law forbidding blind men from driving automobiles.

. . . .

RULE No.361

You are forbidden to allow a horse to ride around in the back seat of your car in Hillsboro, Oregon.

. . . .

RULE No.657

In Connecticut, you can be stopped by the police for biking over 65 miles per hour.

. . . .

RULE No.652

Women may not drive in a house coat, in the state of California.

. . . .

RULE No.631

It's illegal to attach a siren to your bike in Sudbury, Ontario.

. . . .

RULE No.429

In Bermuda, it is illegal to drive
over 20mph.

. . . .

RULE No.427

In Bermuda, cars cannot be wider
than 67 inches (1.7m) or longer
than 169 inches (4.30m).

. . . .

RULE No.417

In Montreal, Canada, "For Sale"
signs are not permitted in the
windows of moving vehicles.

. . . .

RULE No.387

In Utah, birds have the right of
way, on all highways.

. . . .

Chapter 6 - Employment

RULE No.910

In Wacine, Wisconsin, it is illegal to wake a fireman when he is asleep.

. . . .

RULE No.26

In the city of New Orleans, Louisiana, a firefighter on duty cannot curse while performing his duties.

. . . .

RULE No.859

In Danville, Pennsylvania, all fire hydrants must be checked one hour before all fires.

. . . .

RULE No.866

In Charleston, South Carolina, it is
legal for the Fire Department to
blow up your house.

. . . .

RULE No.801

A milk man may not run while on
duty, in St. Louis, Missouri.

. . . .

RULE No.125

In Australia, only licensed
electricians may change a light
bulb.

. . . .

RULE No.307

Michigan state law insists that
dentists officially be classified as
mechanics.

. . . .

RULE No.131

Women who work for the
government of the city of
Guadalajara, Mexico, may not wear
miniskirts or any other provocative
garment during office hours.

. . . .

RULE No.569

In Missouri, it is illegal for an off-
duty fireman to rescue a woman
who is only wearing a nightgown.
In order for her to be rescued, she
must be fully clothed.

. . . .

RULE No.268

A Zeigler, Illinois law states that
only the first 4 firemen reaching a
fire will be paid for their services.

. . . .

RULE No.624

In Rock Springs, Wyoming, it is
illegal for flying instructors to place
their arms around a woman
without a good and lawful reason.

. . . .

Chapter 7 - Entertainment

RULE No.907

Wisconsin State Law made it illegal
to serve apple pie in public
restaurants without cheese.

. . . .

RULE No.915

In Wyoming, you may not take a
picture of a rabbit, from January to
April, without an official permit.

. . . .

RULE No.10

In Arkansas, you cannot sound the
horn in a vehicle after 9pm, at any
place where cold drinks or
sandwiches are served.

. . . .

RULE No.543

If visiting a theatre in the small
village of Winnetka, Illinois, it is
illegal to remove your shoes if your
feet smell.

. . . .

RULE No.25

In Louisville, Kentucky, it is illegal
to walk down the street with an
ice-cream cone in your back
pocket.

. . . .

RULE No.474

In Italy, you can be arrested after
paying for your drinks and food in
any Italian café, if you do not pick
up your receipt and take it at least
40 meters away from the café.

. . . .

RULE No.479

It is illegal for Malaysian restaurant owners to substitute a table napkin with toilet paper.

. . . .

RULE No.888

In Provo, Utah, throwing snowballs will result in a $50 fine.

. . . .

RULE No.893

In Richmond, Virginia, it is illegal to flip a coin in a restaurant to see who pays for coffee.

. . . .

RULE No.32

In Reno, Nevada, marathon dancing or marathon walking is unlawful.

. . . .

RULE No.36

In New York City, it is illegal to
conduct a puppet show in a
window.

. . . .

RULE No.37

In New York City, it is illegal to
allow dancing in an establishment
that sells food, without a cabaret
license.

. . . .

RULE No.871

In Tennessee, it's is a crime to
share your Netflix password.

. . . .

RULE No.875

In Bell buckle, Tennessee, one may
not throw bottles at a tree.

. . . .

RULE No.882

In Galveston, Texas, no person shall inhale fumes from model glue.

. . . .

RULE No.495

In Sweden, it is illegal to train a seal to balance a ball on its nose.

. . . .

RULE No.326

In the state of Nebraska, it is forbidden to picnic twice on the same spot within any 30-day period.

. . . .

RULE No.336

New Hampshire law forbids you to tap your foot, nod your head, or in any way keep time to music in a bar, restaurant, or cafe.

. . . .

RULE No.850

In Eugene, Oregon, it is illegal to
show movies or attend a car race
on Sundays.

. . . .

RULE No.851

In Hood River, Oregon, juggling is
strictly prohibited without a
license.

. . . .

RULE No.828

In the state of North Carolina, it's
against the law to sing off key.

. . . .

RULE No.832

In Devils Lake, North Dakota, you
cannot set off fireworks after
11PM.

. . . .

RULE No.82

In France, between the hours of
8AM and 8PM, 70% of music on
the radio must be by French
artists.

. . . .

RULE No.799

Dancing is strictly prohibited, in the
small city of Purdy, Missouri.

. . . .

RULE No.105

In Canada, 35% of a radio station's
content must be "Canadian
Content".

. . . .

RULE No.106

Residents are not allowed to have
an Internet connection faster than
56k, in Canada.

. . . .

RULE No.776

In the state of Maine, you will be
charged a fine for having
Christmas decorations up, after
January 14th.

. . . .

RULE No.298

It is against the law to play Randy
Newman's "Short People" on the
radio, in the state of Maryland.

. . . .

RULE No.301

Lions may not be taken to the
theatre, in the state of Maryland.

. . . .

RULE No.312

In Minnesota, women
impersonating Santa Claus may
face up to 30 days in jail.

. . . .

RULE No.760

In Burlingame, California, it is
illegal to spit, except on baseball
diamonds.

. . . .

RULE No.763

In Guilford, Connecticut, only white
Christmas lights are allowed for
display.

. . . .

RULE No.134

In Cambodia, water guns may not
be used in New Year's celebrations.
Participants have been known to fill
the water guns with sewage, and
disturb traffic flows with them. The
only punishment for breaking the
rule is the confiscation of the water
gun, nothing more.

. . . .

RULE No.755

Film producers, in the state of
California, must have permission
from a pediatrician before filming a
child under the age of one month.

. . . .

RULE No.512

In San Francisco, California,
picking up used confetti and
throwing it, is banned.

. . . .

RULE No.700

In the state of Iowa, one-armed
piano players must perform for
free.

. . . .

RULE No.242

In Florida, a special law prohibits
unmarried women from
parachuting on Sunday, or she
shall risk arrest, fines, and/or jail.

. . . .

RULE No.243

In Florida, you are breaking the law if you skateboard without a license.

. . . .

RULE No.273

In Gary, Indiana, it is illegal to attend the theatre within four hours of eating garlic.

. . . .

RULE No.649

In Baldwin Park, California, no one is allowed to ride a bicycle in a swimming pool.

. . . .

RULE No.362

In Hood River, Oregon, it is prohibited to juggle without a license.

. . . .

RULE No.661

Silly strings are banned in
Southington, Connecticut.

. . . .

RULE No.634

It's illegal to build big snowmen in
Souris, Canada.

. . . .

RULE No.505

In California, a law created in 1925
prohibits women from wiggling
their bottoms while dancing.

. . . .

RULE No.583

In the state of New York, it is
illegal to start any kind of public
performance, show, play or game
until after 1:05pm.

. . . .

RULE No.589

A 1995, city ordinance in
Sandusky, Ohio outlawed trick or
treating by anyone older than 14.

. . . .

RULE No.626

Under Illinois state law, it is a
violation to build a snowman taller
than 10 feet (3 meters).

Chapter 8 - Fashion

RULE No.261

In the suburb of Gurnee, Illinois, if you are a woman weighing more than 200 pounds, you are forbidden from wearing shorts when you go horse riding.

. . . .

RULE No.262

Women in Joliet, Illinois can be jailed for trying on more than 6 dresses in any one shop.

. . . .

RULE No.12

In the state of Arkansas, school teachers who bob their hair will not get a raise.

. . . .

RULE No.535

To be seen in public wearing only
swimming trunks and little else is
an act of indecency, in the state of
Hawaii.

. . . .

RULE No.536

In the large city of Honolulu, HI, it
is illegal for any woman to be on
Waikiki Beach or in the water
without wearing modesty shoes or
lightweight bathing footwear.

. . . .

RULE No.475

On entry to the Vatican, in Italy,
you can be ejected if your clothes
are not suitable.

. . . .

RULE No.477

In Laos, women are not allowed to
show their toes in public.

. . . .

RULE No.478

In Magadascar, it's illegal for pregnant women to wear hats.

. . . .

RULE No.394

In the state of Vermont, women must obtain written permission from their husbands in order to wear false teeth.

. . . .

RULE No.869

In Myrtle Beach, South Carolina, persons may not change clothes in a gas station without permission of the owner.

. . . .

RULE No.49

In Miday, Tennessee, it is illegal to wear socks with sandals.

. . . .

RULE No.858

In the town of Connellsville, Pennsylvani, one's pants may be worn no lower than 5 inches below the waist.

. . . .

RULE No.860

In Morrisville, Pennsylvania, it is required that a woman have a permit to wear cosmetics.

. . . .

RULE No.863

In Providence, Rhode Island, it is illegal to wear transparent clothing.

. . . .

RULE No.867

In the foothills of Fountain Inn, South Carolina, horses are to wear pants at all times.

. . . .

RULE No.837

In the state of Oklahoma, it's
illegal to wear your boots to bed.

. . . .

RULE No.820

In New Mexico, women may walk
in public topless, provided they
have their nipples covered.

. . . .

RULE No.825

In the state of New York, slippers
are not to be worn after 10:00 PM.

. . . .

RULE No.826

In New York, it is illegal for a
woman to be on the street wearing
"body hugging clothing".

. . . .

RULE No.830

In the state of North Dakota, it is illegal to lie down and fall asleep with your shoes on.

. . . .

RULE No.321

In the town of Saco, Missouri, women are forbidden from wearing hats that might frighten timid persons, children or animals.

. . . .

RULE No.215

In Tucson, Arizona, it is unlawful for women to wear trousers.

. . . .

RULE No.116

In Australia, It is illegal to wear hot pink pants after midday Sunday.

. . . .

RULE No.117

In Australia, you must have a
neck-to-knee swimsuit, in order to
swim at Brighton Beach.

. . . .

RULE No.120

In Australia, It is illegal to roam
the streets wearing black clothes,
felt shoes and black shoe polish on
your face as these items are the
tools of a cat burglar.

. . . .

RULE No.127

In Italy, a man may be arrested for
wearing a skirt.

. . . .

RULE No.761

In Carmel, California, a man
cannot go outside while wearing a
jacket and pants that do not
match.

. . . .

RULE No.762

In Carmel, California, women may
not wear high heels while in the
city limits.

. . . .

RULE No.772

It is illegal to wear sagging pants
in Collinsville, Illinois.

. . . .

RULE No.448

In Finland, at one time, Donald
Duck comics were banned because
Donald didn't wear any pants.

. . . .

RULE No.152

In Switzerland, clothes may not be
hung to dry on Sunday.

. . . .

RULE No.161

In Thailand, it is illegal to leave your house if you are not wearing underwear.

. . . .

RULE No.568

Women are prohibited from wearing corsets in Merryville, Missouri because "the privilege of admiring the curvaceous, unencumbered body of young women should not be denied to the normal, red-blooded American male".

. . . .

RULE No.743

In Australia, men are free to cross-dress, as long as their dresses are not strapless.

. . . .

RULE No.515

In Gunnison, Colorado, it is illegal
for a man to either hide his wife's
lipstick or throw it away.

. . . .

RULE No.181

In the state of Nevada, it is illegal
to use x-rays to determine shoe
size.

. . . .

RULE No.596

Wearing 'puke green' colored socks
on a Sunday is prohibited under
the Oregon State Constitution.

. . . .

RULE No.715

In the state of Maine, shoelaces
must be tied while walking down
the street.

. . . .

RULE No.721

In the state of Maryland, it is a
park rule violation to be in a public
park with a sleeveless shirt.

. . . .

RULE No.445

In Ecuador, a woman may legally
dance in public wearing nothing
more than a piece of gauze
covering her belly button.

. . . .

RULE No.467

In Israel, no person is allowed to
dress or undress in a room with the
light switched on.

. . . .

RULE No.691

In the state of Illinois, it is unlawful
to change clothes in an automobile
with the curtains drawn, except in
case of fire.

. . . .

RULE No.200

In Kentucky, no female shall
appear in a bathing suit, on any
highway within the state unless
she be escorted by at least 2

officers or unless she be armed
with a club.

. . . .

RULE No.206

In Japan, women cannot wear
pants to work.

. . . .

RULE No.281

In Lang, Kansas, it is against the
law to ride a mule down Main
Street in August, unless, of course,
the said mule is wearing a straw
hat.

. . . .

RULE No.282

You can't carry bees around in your
hat on the city streets, in
Lawrence, Kansas.

. . . .

RULE No.283

In Natoma, Kansas, it is illegal to
throw a knife at anyone wearing a
striped shirt.

. . . .

RULE No.349

In Charlotte, North Carolina,
women must have their bodies
covered by at least 16 yards of
cloth at all times.

. . . .

RULE No.368

In Morrisville, Pennsylvania,
women need a permit to wear
cosmetics.

. . . .

RULE No.667

In the state of Delaware, it is
illegal to wear pants that are "firm
fitting" around the waist.

. . . .

RULE No.650

In Blythe, California, you are not
permitted to wear cowboy boots

unless you already own at least 2
cows.

. . . .

RULE No.639

In Anniston, Alabama, you may not
wear blue jeans down Noble
Street.

. . . .

RULE No.633

Taxi drivers cannot wear t-shirts in
Halifax, Nova Scotia.

. . . .

RULE No.413

In St. Croix, Wisconsin, women are
not allowed to wear anything red,
in public.

. . . .

RULE No.420

In the United Kingdom, no boy
under the age of ten may see a
naked mannequin.

. . . .

RULE No.423

In Bermuda, women must not wear
skirts shorter than 8 inches (20cm)
above the knee in public places.

. . . .

RULE No.527

In the state of Florida, it is illegal
for women to expose more than
2/3rds of her bottom at the beach.
If the bikini doesn't cover at least
one third of her rear end, a $500
fine can be imposed.

. . . .

RULE No.563

In Michigan, it is against the law
for a lady to lift her skirt more than
6 inches while walking through a
mud puddle.

. . . .

RULE No.590

A law was passed banning women
from wearing patent leather shoes
in Cleveland, Ohio, in case a man
might catch a glimpse of
something he shouldn't.

. . . .

RULE No.629

It's a crime to fall asleep while
wearing a fur coat under the
Washington State Constitution.

Chapter 9 - Food

RULE No.263

In Chicago, Illinois, it is against the
law to eat in a place that is on fire.

. . . .

RULE No.267

In Oak Park, Illinois, it is against
the law to fry more than 100
doughnuts in a single day.

. . . .

RULE No.905

In the state of West Virginia,
roadkill may be taken home for
supper.

. . . .

RULE No.540

In Idaho, you cannot buy onions
after dark, without a special permit
from the Sheriff.

. . . .

RULE No.900

In the state of Washington, you
cannot buy meat, of any kind, on
Sunday.

. . . .

RULE No.469

In Israel, pork cannot be legally
sold.

. . . .

RULE No.482

In Peru, the use of chili sauce and
similar hot spices added to prison
food is outlawed. These items are
thought to be aphrodisiacs and

therefore unsuitable for pent-up
inmates.

. . . .

RULE No.895

In the state of Washington, it is illegal to attach a vending machine to a utility pole, without prior consent from the utility company.

. . . .

RULE No.898

In the state of Washington, all lollipops are banned.

. . . .

RULE No.34

In Conada, New York, it is prohibited to serve margarine as a butter substitute, at a public eating place, unless it is ordered by the customer.

. . . .

RULE No.872

It is legal to gather and consume roadkill, in Tennessee.

. . . .

RULE No.44

In Oklahoma, it is illegal to take a bite out of someone's hamburger without first asking permission.

. . . .

RULE No.492

In Saudi Arabia, a wife can divorce her husband if he fails to keep her supplied with coffee.

. . . .

RULE No.339

In the state of New Jersey, it is against the law for a person to slurp soup.

. . . .

RULE No.62

In the U.K., it is illegal for a lady to eat chocolates on a public conveyance.

. . . .

RULE No.561

It is illegal to deface milk cartons,
in the state of Massachusetts.

. . . .

RULE No.852

In Marion, Oregon, you cannot eat
a doughnut and walk backwards on
a city street.

. . . .

RULE No.80

In France, in ads for products that
contain salt or sugar, it's
mandatory to include that you
should exercise and eat at least 5
fruits and vegetables a day.

. . . .

RULE No.167

In California, a frog that dies
during a frog-jumping contest
cannot be eaten.

. . . .

RULE No.172

In the state of Idaho, cannibalism
is prohibited. It is permitted,
however, to willfully ingest the
flesh or blood of a human being.

. . . .

RULE No.823

You may not carry a lunchbox
down Main Street in Las Cruces,
Minnesota.

. . . .

RULE No.831

In North Dakota, beer and pretzels
cannot be served at the same time,
in any bar or restaurant.

. . . .

RULE No.89

In Denmark, one may not be
charged for food at an inn unless
that person, by his or her own
opinion, is full.

. . . .

RULE No.91

In Denmark, restaurants may not charge for water unless it is accompanied by another item such as ice or a lemon slice.

. . . .

RULE No.812

Doughnut holes may not be sold, in the town of Lehigh, Nebraska.

. . . .

RULE No.213

In the state of Arizona, it is unlawful to refuse a person a glass of water.

. . . .

RULE No.233

In Connecticut, in order for a pickle to be officially considered a pickle, it must bounce.

. . . .

RULE No.786

In the state of Massachusetts, tomatoes may not be used in the production of clam chowder.

. . . .

RULE No.774

In Derby, Kansas, hitting a vending machine that steals your money, is illegal.

. . . .

RULE No.775

In Louisianna, it is a $500 fine to instruct a pizza delivery man to deliver a pizza to your friend, without them knowing.

. . . .

RULE No.140

In Singapore, the sale of gum is prohibited.

. . . .

RULE No.454

In the United Kingdom, anyone caught sticking chewing gum to the underside of a seat on the upper deck of a bus can be detained in custody for 24 hours, if they are caught.

. . . .

RULE No.572

In Nebraska, it is unlawful to eat fried chicken while walking down the sidewalk.

. . . .

RULE No.575

In the state of New Jersey, cabbage cannot be sold on a Sunday.

. . . .

RULE No.731

In St. Cloud, Minnesota,
hamburgers may not be eaten on
Sundays.

. . . .

RULE No.604

In the state of Rhode Island, it is illegal for farmers to plant corn in March.

. . . .

RULE No.605

In Tennessee, the sale of bologna (sandwich meat) is prohibited on Sundays.

. . . .

RULE No.197

It's against the law, in the state of Vermont, for vagrants to procure food by force.

. . . .

RULE No.275

Iowa state law makes it illegal to have a rotten egg in your possession.

. . . .

RULE No.279

It is against the law to eat snakes
on Sunday, in Kansas.

. . . .

RULE No.342

In Trenton, New Jersey, it is
unlawful to throw a bad pickle in
the street.

. . . .

RULE No.381

In the state of Texas, it is illegal to
milk another person's cow.

. . . .

RULE No.637

You may not have an ice cream
cone in your back pocket, at any
time in the state of Alabama.

. . . .

RULE No.388

In Salt Lake City, Utah, you cannot give away fish on Sunday, or on a public holiday.

. . . .

RULE No.414

In Quebec, Canada, margarine producers cannot make their margarine yellow.

. . . .

RULE No.419

In the U.K., any person found breaking a boiled egg at the narrow end will be sentenced to 24 hours, in the village stocks.

. . . .

RULE No.500

If caught stealing citrus fruit in Yuma, Arizona, you may be administered castor oil as a punishment.

. . . .

RULE No.622

In the state of West Virginia, you
can be imprisoned for cooking
cabbage or sauerkraut, due to the
horrendous smell.

. . . .

Chapter 10 - Games

RULE No.909

In La Crosse, Wisconsin, it is illegal
to play checkers in public.

. . . .

RULE No.38

In North Carolina, it is illegal to
hold more than 2 sessions of bingo
per week. Also, each session
cannot exceed 5 hours.

. . . .

RULE No.807

In Excelsior Springs, Montana,
balls may not be thrown within the
city limits.

. . . .

RULE No.809

All pool tables must be able to be viewed from the street outside a billiard hall where they are located, in the town of Kalispell, Montana.

. . . .

RULE No.115

All electronic games are banned, in Greece.

. . . .

RULE No.294

In the state of Maine, the most money one can legally win by gambling is $3.00.

. . . .

RULE No.139

In Singapore, Bungee jumping is illegal.

. . . .

RULE No.164

In Alabama, it's illegal to purchase, possess or train a bear for the purposes of bear wrestling.

. . . .

RULE No.177

In the state of Minnesota, any game in which participants attempt to capture a greased or oiled pig, is illegal.

. . . .

RULE No.520

A local ordinance bans people in Woodville, Connecticut from playing Scrabble while waiting for a politician to speak.

. . . .

RULE No.436

In Alberta, Canada, you cannot use dice to play the game of craps.

. . . .

RULE No.240

In the state of Delaware,
unmarried women, who parachute
on Sundays, may be jailed.

. . . .

RULE No.679

Goldfish may not be given away, to
entice someone to enter a game of
bingo, in the state of Georgia.

. . . .

RULE No.675

In Georgia, persons under the age
of 16 may not play pinball after
11:00 PM.

. . . .

RULE No.593

It is illegal for a baseball team to
hit the ball over the fence or out of
the ballpark, in the state of
Oklahoma.

. . . .

Chapter 11 - Guns and Ammo

RULE No.21

In the state of Illinois, anyone
under the age of 18 can get a gun
permit, with their parent's or
guardian's consent.

. . . .

RULE No.481

In Paraguay, dueling is legal,
provided both parties are
registered blood donors.

. . . .

RULE No.403

In Seattle, Washington, residents
may not carry concealed weapons
longer than six feet.

. . . .

RULE No.50

In Kaysville, Utah, it is illegal to donate a nuclear weapon but you can own one.

. . . .

RULE No.57

In the United Kingdom, it is legal to shoot a Scotsman, except on Sundays.

. . . .

RULE No.549

In Chicago, Illinois, a hat pin is legally regarded as being a concealed weapon.

. . . .

RULE No.77

In Germany, a pillow can be considered a passive weapon.

. . . .

RULE No.87

In France, an ashtray is considered
to be a deadly weapon.

. . . .

RULE No.797

Minors are not allowed to purchase
cap pistols. However, they may
buy shotguns, in Kansas City,
Missouri.

. . . .

RULE No.214

In Arizona, when being attacked by
a criminal or a burglar, you may
only protect yourself with the same
weapon that the other person
possesses.

. . . .

RULE No.785

In the state of Massachusetts,
shooting ranges may not set up
targets that resemble human
beings.

. . . .

RULE No.183

In New Jersey, it is illegal to wear
a bullet proof vest while
committing murder, manslaughter,
robbery, or sexual assault.

. . . .

Chapter 12 - Hair

RULE No.542

In Illinois, barbers are banned from using their fingers to apply shaving cream to a patron's face.

. . . .

RULE No.18

In Atlanta, Georgia, it is illegal to let your pubic hair grow past 6 inches.

. . . .

RULE No.27

In the state of Michigan, it is illegal for a woman to get her hair cut without her husband's permission.

. . . .

RULE No.327

In Omaha, Nebraska, barbers are
forbidden from shaving their
customers' chests.

. . . .

RULE No.329

In Waterloo, Nebraska, barbers are
forbidden from eating onions
between 7am and 7pm.

. . . .

RULE No.332

Men who wear moustaches in the
tiny town of Eureka, Nevada
(population approx. 660) are
forbidden from kissing women.

. . . .

RULE No.553

In Louisiana, a bill was once instigated in the State House of Representatives that fixed a ceiling on the price of haircuts for bald men at 25 cents.

. . . .

RULE No.559

In Massachusetts, it is illegal to have a goatee beard, unless you first pay a special license fee for the privilege of wearing one in public.

. . . .

RULE No.836

In the state of Oklahoma, females are forbidden from doing their own hair, without being licensed by the state.

. . . .

RULE No.324

It is illegal for a mother to give her daughter a perm without a license, in the state of Nebraska.

. . . .

RULE No.813

A man is not allowed to run around with a shaved chest, in Omaha, Nebraska.

. . . .

RULE No.212

In Anchorage, Alaska, every year, all male residents must grow beards from the 5th of January to the middle of February, when a celebration called the Fur Rendezvous is held.

. . . .

RULE No.580

In New Mexico, females are
prohibited from appearing in public
unshaven.

. . . .

RULE No.244

In the state of Florida, women may
be fined for falling asleep under a
hair dryer, as can the salon owner.

. . . .

RULE No.313

Every man in Brainerd, Minnesota
is required by law to grow a beard.

. . . .

RULE No.347

If you are Santa Claus in New York
City, by law, you must make sure
that the whiskers you wear in
public are fireproof.

. . . .

RULE No.367

Beards more than 2.5 feet long are
forbidden by law in Altoona,
Pennsylvania.

. . . .

RULE No.386

In Mesquite, Texas, it is illegal for
children to have unusual haircuts.

. . . .

RULE No.410

It is unlawful to cut a woman's
hair, in the state of Wisconsin.

. . . .

RULE No.530

It is illegal for a barber to advertise
his prices, in the state of Georgia.

. . . .

Chapter 13 - Health

RULE No.493

In Saudi Arabia, male doctors may
not examine women and female
doctors cannot examine men.

. . . .

RULE No.773

In the state of Iowa, a board was
created to regulate hearing aids.

. . . .

RULE No.453

In the U.K., a pregnant woman can
legally urinate anywhere she wants
to, including in a policeman's
helmet.

. . . .

RULE No.144

In Singapore, failure to flush a
public toilet after use may result in
very hefty fines.

. . . .

RULE No.698

In the state of Indiana, a person
must get a referral from a licensed
physician if he or she wishes to see
a hypnotist, unless the desired
procedure is to quit smoking or
lose weight.

. . . .

Chapter 14 - Hunting

RULE No.704

It is illegal to catch fish with your bare hands, in Kansas.

. . . .

RULE No.705

In the state of Kansas, the state game rule prohibits the use of mules to hunt ducks.

. . . .

RULE No.6

It is illegal to shoot any game other than whales from a moving vehicle, in the state of Tennessee.

. . . .

RULE No.259

In Chicago, Illinois, it is against the law to fish in your pajamas.

. . . .

RULE No.818

In New Jersey, it is against the law for a man to knit during fishing season.

. . . .

RULE No.257

In the state of Idaho, it is against the law to go fishing while sitting on a camel.

. . . .

RULE No.364

Oregon state law forbids the use of canned corn in fishing.

. . . .

RULE No.375

In Tennessee, it is against the law
to use a lasso to catch a fish.

. . . .

RULE No.404

In the state of West Virginia, it is
illegal for a person to persuade
another person to kill a frog for
him.

. . . .

RULE No.39

It is illegal to fish for whales on
Sundays, in the state of Ohio.

. . . .

RULE No.219

In the state of California, it is
unlawful to set a mousetrap unless
you have a hunting license.

. . . .

RULE No.510

In Los Angeles, California, it is forbidden to hunt moths under a streetlight.

. . . .

RULE No.682

In the state of Idaho, residents may not fish from a giraffe's back.

. . . .

RULE No.621

It is illegal to catch a fish by throwing a rock at it, in the state of Washington.

. . . .

Chapter 15 - Hygiene

RULE No.703

In the small town of McLough,
Kansas, it is illegal to wash your
false teeth in a public drinking
fountain.

. . . .

RULE No.903

In Waldron Island, Washington, no
structure shall contain more than
two toilets that use potable water
for flushing.

. . . .

RULE No.892

In Culpeper, Virginia, no one may
wash a mule on the sidewalk.

. . . .

RULE No.896

In the state of Washington, no person may walk about in public if he or she has the common cold.

. . . .

RULE No.395

In Virginia, bathtubs are forbidden in the house; they must be kept in the garden.

. . . .

RULE No.43

In the state of Oklahoma, it is illegal to have a sleeping donkey in your bathtub.

. . . .

RULE No.337

In the state of New Hampshire, citizens may not relieve themselves while looking up, on Sundays.

. . . .

RULE No.855

In the town of Stanfield, Oregon, cloth towel dispensers are banned from restrooms.

. . . .

RULE No.64

In the United Kingdom, it is legal for a male to urinate in public, as long as it is on the rear wheel of his motor vehicle and his right hand is on the vehicle.

. . . .

RULE No.555

It is illegal to post an advertisement on a public urinal in Boston, Massachusetts.

. . .

RULE No.844

In Wynona, Oklahoma, clothes may not be washed in bird baths.

. . . .

RULE No.75

In Israel, it is illegal to pick you nose on the Sabbath.

. . . .

RULE No.234

In Connecticut, it is unlawful to dispose of used razor blades.

. . . .

RULE No.791

In the state of Minnesota, all bathtubs must not have feet.

. . . .

RULE No.292

In New Orleans, Louisiana, it is considered 'simple assault' to bite someone; and if the biter has false teeth, then it is 'aggravated assault'.

. . . .

RULE No.296

In Waterville, Maine, it is against the law to blow your nose in public.

. . . .

RULE No.304

In Boston, Massachusetts, it is against the law to take a bath unless ordered to do so by a physician.

. . . .

RULE No.769

In Eagle, Idaho, dirt may not be swept from one's house into the street.

. . . .

RULE No.455

In Scotland, if a stranger knocks on your door and requires the use of your commode, you must allow them to enter.

. . . .

RULE No.497

In the state of Alabama, boogers
may not be flicked into the wind.

. . . .

RULE No.752

In Mohave County, Arizona, a
decree declares that anyone
caught stealing soap must wash
himself with it until it is all used
up.

. . . .

RULE No.753

In Tombstone, Arizona, it is illegal
for men and women over the age
of 18 to have less than one missing
tooth visible, when smiling.

. . . .

RULE No.147

In Singapore, it is illegal to pee in
an elevator.

. . . .

RULE No.155

In Switzerland, it is illegal to flush
the toilet after 10pm.

. . . .

RULE No.156

In Switzerland, a man may not
relieve himself while standing up,
after 10pm.

. . . .

RULE No.567

In Minnesota, it is illegal to hang
men and women's underwear on
the same washing line.

. . . .

RULE No.508

In Los Angeles, California, you
cannot bathe two babies in the
same bathtub at the same time.

. . . .

RULE No.723

In the state of Massachusetts, it is
illegal to go to bed without first
having a full bath.

. . . .

RULE No.600

In Pennsylvania, a special cleaning
ordinance bans housewives from
concealing dirt and dust under a
rug in a dwelling.

. . . .

RULE No.603

In the state of Rhode Island, it is
illegal to sell toothbrushes on
Sunday.

. . . .

RULE No.192

Bowling Green, Ohio created a law
making it a crime to sleep within
500 feet of urine or feces that
hasn't been properly deposited.

. . . .

RULE No.693

In the state of Indiana, baths may
not be taken between the months
of October and March.

. . . .

RULE No.285

In the state of Kentucky, every
person must take a bath at least
once a year.

. . . .

RULE No.348

In Asheville, North Carolina, it is
illegal to sneeze on city streets.

. . . .

RULE No.648

In San Francisco, California, it is
illegal to spray people's clothing
with saliva spewed out of your
mouth.

. . . .

RULE No.408

In the state of Wisconsin, only one
person may take a bath in a tub at
one time.

. . . .

RULE No.418

In Etobicoke, Canada, bylaw states
that no more than 3.5 inches of
water is allowed in a bathtub.

. . . .

Chapter 16 - Law Enforcement

RULE No.264

In the state of Illinois, your pet
animal can be sent to jail. A
monkey once served 5 days in a
Chicago jail for shoplifting.

. . . .

RULE No.468

In Israel, there is no legal way for
any man named Cohen to marry a
divorced woman.

. . . .

RULE No.480

In Paraguay, if a man catches his
wife in bed with somebody else, he
is legally entitled to kill his wife
and her lover, but only if he acts
immediately.

. . . .

RULE No.886

In Utah, it is illegal to cause a
catastrophe.

. . . .

RULE No.401

In the state of Washington, it's
illegal to pretend that your parents
are rich, when they're not.

. . . .

RULE No.40

In Dayton, Ohio, homeless people
must apply for and carry a license
to beg on the street.

. . . .

RULE No.47

In Abbeville, South Carolina, it is illegal to spit in the town square.

. . . .

RULE No.330

In Nevada, it is still legal to hang someone for shooting your dog on your property.

. . . .

RULE No.338

In the state of New Jersey, it is forbidden to frown at a police officer.

. . . .

RULE No.856

In the town of Yamhill, Oregon, it is illegal to predict the future.

. . . .

RULE No.861

In the state of Rhode Island, it is illegal to bite another man's leg off.

. . . .

RULE No.868

In Hilton head, South Carolina, one commits a nuisance if he or she leaves a large amount of trash in their own vehicle.

. . . .

RULE No.59

In the United Kingdom, damaging grass is illegal.

. . . .

RULE No.63

In the U.K., you need a license to keep a lunatic.

. . . .

RULE No.547

In the state of Illinois, it is against
the law to eavesdrop.

. . . .

RULE No.556

A state law forbids cooling one's
feet by hanging them out of the
window, in the state of
Massachusetts.

. . . .

RULE No.560

In the state of Massachusetts,
snoring is strictly forbidden unless
all bedroom windows are closed
and securely locked.

. . . .

RULE No.849

In Beaverton, Oregon, you must
buy a $10 permit to be allowed to
install a burglar alarm.

. . . .

RULE No.78

In Germany, it is illegal to wear a mask.

. . . .

RULE No.824

In New York, it is illegal to congregate in public, with two or more people, while wearing a mask or any face covering, which disguises your identity.

. . . .

RULE No.827

In the state of North Carolina, it is a felony to steal more than $1000 of grease.

. . . .

RULE No.85

In France, it is illegal to take photos of police officers or police

vehicles, even if they are just in
the background.

. . . .

RULE No.93

In Denmark, an attempt to escape
from prison is not illegal. However,
if one is caught, he is required to
serve out the remainder of his
term.

. . . .

RULE No.808

No item may be thrown across a
street, in the town of Helena,
Montana.

. . . .

RULE No.104

Comic books which depict any
illegal acts are banned, in Canada.

. . . .

RULE No.230

In Los Angeles, California, it is
against the law to cry on the
witness stand.

. . . .

RULE No.293

In Louisiana, it is illegal to rob a
bank and then shoot at the bank
teller with a water pistol.

. . . .

RULE No.303

In the state of Massachusetts,
peanuts may not be eaten in court.

. . . .

RULE No.749

In Anchorage, Alaska, it is illegal to
string a wire across any road.

. . . .

RULE No.750

In Arizona, any misdemeanor
committed while wearing a red
mask is considered a felony.

. . . .

RULE No.751

In the state of Arizona, there is a possible 25 years in prison for cutting down a cactus.

. . . .

RULE No.146

In Singapore, if you are convicted of littering 3 times, you will have to clean the streets on Sundays with a bib, saying, "I am a litterer".

. . . .

RULE No.154

In Switzerland, it is considered an offense to mow your lawn on Sundays, because it causes too much noise.

. . . .

RULE No.578

In Quemado, New Mexico, a
newspaper can be fined if it
misspells a person's name, in print.

. . . .

RULE No.735

In Missouri, single men between
the ages of 21 and 50 must pay an
annual tax of one dollar.

. . . .

RULE No.178

In the state of Mississippi, using
profanity in front of two or more
people is illegal. Up to 30 days in
jail or a $100 fine, or both.

. . . .

RULE No.518

In Denver, Colorado, it is illegal to
lend your vacuum cleaner to your
next-door neighbor.

. . . .

RULE No.610

In Texas, the law requires criminals to give their victims 24 hour's notice, either orally or in writing, explaining the nature of the crime to be committed, before committing the crime.

. . . .

RULE No.190

According to a Bowling Green, Ohio city ordinance, it's illegal to sit on top of picnic tables, fences or any other type of railing in the city's public park.

. . . .

RULE No.191

The city of Bowling Green, Ohio also outlaws climbing trees in the parks. In addition, a person must get approval from a city park director if s(he) wants to bring a helium balloon inside the park.

. . . .

RULE No.274

In the small town of Hammond,
Indiana, if you stand still and look
lazy, you can legally be classified
as a loiterer.

. . . .

RULE No.676

In Georgia, to spit on sidewalks
after dark is illegal, during daylight
hours it is acceptable.

. . . .

RULE No.642

In the state of Arizona, it is illegal
to manufacture imitation cocaine.

. . . .

RULE No.346

In New York City, it is disorderly
conduct for one man to greet
another on the street by placing
the end of his thumb against the
tip of his nose, at the same time
extending and wiggling the fingers
of his hand.

. . . .

RULE No.352

If you meet a man in the state of North Dakota who is wanted for a felony and he refuses to go with you to a police station, you are legally entitled to shoot him!

. . . .

RULE No.673

In Atlanta, Georgia, it is illegal for one man to carry another man on his back.

. . . .

RULE No.635

In the United States, it is illegal to leave your cell phone unlocked.

. . . .

RULE No.388

In Utah, a husband is responsible for every criminal act committed

by his wife while she is in his
presence.

. . . .

RULE No.531

It is illegal to spread false rumors,
in the state of Georgia.

. . . .

RULE No.562

The law in Rochester, Michigan
states that anyone bathing in
public must have their bathing suit
inspected by a police officer.

. . . .

Chapter 17 - Lifestyle

RULE No.260

It is illegal to take a French poodle
to the opera, in Chicago, Illinois.

. . . .

RULE No.11

In Arkansas, a man can legally
beat his wife but not more than
once a month.

. . . .

RULE No.17

In the state of Connecticut, it is
illegal for unmarried couples to live
together.

. . . .

RULE No.19

In Honolulu, Hawaii, it is illegal to sing loudly outside after sunset.

. . . .

RULE No.472

In Naples, Italy, a man is allowed to have as many mistresses as he wishes, provided that his wife knows, and that he can afford to maintain his wife and mistress in the lifestyle to which they are accustomed.

. . . .

RULE No.887

In the city of Logan, Utah, women may not swear.

. . . .

RULE No.891

In the state of Virginia, it is illegal to tickle women.

. . . .

RULE No.28

In Grand Haven, Michigan, it is illegal to keep your garage door open for more than 3 hours.

. . . .

RULE No.394

In Vermont, it is against the law to whistle underwater.

. . . .

RULE No.52

In the state of Wyoming, it is illegal to possess or display red or black flags.

. . . .

RULE No.488

In Jeddah, Saudi Arabia, in 1979, women were banned by royal decree from using hotel swimming pools.

. . . .

RULE No.490

In Saudi Arabia, it is against the law for a woman to appear in public without a male relative or guardian present.

. . . .

RULE No.494

In Sweden, it is illegal for parents to shame or insult their children.

. . . .

RULE No.331

Everyone walking on the streets of Elko, Nevada is required to wear a mask.

. . . .

RULE No.853

In Portland, Oregon, you cannot wear roller skates in restrooms.

. . . .

RULE No.56

In the United Kingdom, divorces
are outlawed.

. . . .

RULE No.552

In Kentucky, marrying the same
man 4 times is illegal.

. . . .

RULE No.848

In the state of Oregon, dishes must
drip dry.

. . . .

RULE No.73

In Israel, loud voices or big lights
are not allowed on weekends.

. . . .

RULE No.322

It is a criminal act for a wife to open her husband's mail, in the state of Montana.

. . . .

RULE No.798

Minors can buy rolling paper and tobacco but not lighters, in the city of Marceline, Missouri.

. . . .

RULE No.802

No person may own a PVC pipe, in the suburb of University City, Missouri.

. . . .

RULE No.804

It is illegal to use speed-dial in the city phone system, in Billings, Montana.

....

RULE No.805

In Excelsior Springs, Montana,
hard objects may not be thrown by
hand.

. . . .

RULE No.101

To go to college you must be
intelligent, in China.

. . . .

RULE No.108

You may not paint a ladder as it
will be slippery when wet, in
Canada.

. . . .

RULE No.207

In Iceland, it is illegal to blow on
lampposts.

. . . .

RULE No.208

In Samoa, it is illegal to forget your
wife's birthday.

. . . .

RULE No.792

In Minneapolis, Minnesota, people
are forbidden from walking in
and/or down alleyways.

. . . .

RULE No.795

In Columbia, Missouri, clotheslines
are banned, but clothes may be
draped over a fence.

. . . .

RULE No.118

In Australia, Children may not
purchase cigarettes but they may
smoke them.

. . . .

RULE No.121

In Australia, It is illegal to walk on
the right hand side of a footpath.

. . . .

RULE No.299

In Baltimore, Maryland, it is illegal
to wash or scrub sinks, no matter
how dirty they get.

. . .

RULE No.305

If you live in Southbridge,
Massachusetts, it is against the law
to read books or newspapers after
8pm in the streets.

. . . .

RULE No.766

All citizens in Acworth, Georgia
must own a rake.

. . . .

RULE No.771

In the state of Illinois, the English
language is not to be spoken.

. . . .

RULE No.447

In Finland, to get married, the law
stipulates that both the man and
woman are able to read.

. . . .

RULE No.459

In Guinea, it is illegal to give the
name 'Monica' to a baby.

. . . .

RULE No.754

In the state of Arkansas, iIt is
strictly prohibited to pronounce
"Arkansas" incorrectly.

. . . .

RULE No.145

In Singapore, it is illegal to come
within 50 meters of a pedestrian
crossing marker on any street.

. . . .

RULE No.151

In Charrat, a small town in
Switzerland, it is illegal to ride
down hills, with a bike.

. . . .

RULE No.571

In the state of Nebraska, spitting
into the wind is illegal.

. . . .

RULE No.582

In the state of New York, it is
against the law for children to pick
up or collect cigarette and cigar
butts.

....

RULE No.741

In a 2013 China law, it is illegal for children not to visit their parents often.

. . . .

RULE No.741

In Bangladesh, children who are 15 or older can be sent to jail for cheating on final exams.

. . . .

RULE No.515

In San Francisco, California, it is illegal to clean one's car with used underwear.

. . . .

RULE No.182

In the state of New Hampshire, it is illegal to collect seaweed at night.

. . . .

RULE No.597

In the state of Oregon, before
entering the Pacific Ocean,
swimmers must remove their
socks.

. . . .

RULE No.193

In Joliet, Illinois, it is illegal to
mispronounce the name Joliet.

. . . .

RULE No.198

It is against the law in Pueblo,
Colorado, to raise or permit a
dandelion to grow within the city
limits.

. . . .

RULE No.463

Among the Malagasy tribe in India,
if a son is taller than his father, the
father has to pay his son either in
money or give him an ox.

. . . .

RULE No.684

In the state of Idaho, a person
may not be seen in public without
a smile on their face.

. . . .

RULE No.685

In the state of Illinois, you may be
arrested for vagrancy if you do not
have at least one dollar bill on your
person.

. . . .

RULE No.686

One may not pee in his neighbor's
mouth in Champaign, Illinois.

. . . .

RULE No.695

In the state of Indiana, the value
of Pi is 3.

. . . .

RULE No.250

In the state of Florida, you may not fart in a public place after 6pm on Thursdays.

. . . .

RULE No.249

In Florida, you are not allowed to break more than three dishes per day, or chip the edges of more than four cups and/or saucers.

. . . .

RULE No.658

In Devon, Connecticut, it is illegal to walk backwards after sunset.

. . . .

RULE No.653

In Denver, Colorado, it is illegal to lend your vacuum cleaner to your next-door neighbor.

....

RULE No.289

It is against the law to gargle in public, in the state of Louisiana.

. . . .

RULE No.290

In the state of Louisiana, you could end up in jail for up to a year for making a false promise.

. . . .

RULE No.343

The Merriam-Webster Collegiate Dictionary is banned in Carlsbad, New Mexico.

. . . .

RULE No.365

In Portland, Oregon, it is illegal to wear roller skates in public toilets.

. . . .

RULE No.369

It is illegal to smoke a pipe after sunset in Newport, Pennsylvania.

. . . .

RULE No.677

Georgia has a state law prohibiting people from saying "oh boy" in public.

. . . .

RULE No.671

The use of profanity over the phone is illegal, in Columbus, Georgia.

. . . .

RULE No.434

It is illegal to swear in French in Montreal, Canada; although, there are no restrictions on swearing in English.

. . . .

RULE No.501

The Paitue Indian Reservation in
the state of California forbids a
mother-in-law to spend more than
30 days a year with her children.

. . . .

RULE No.532

In the state of Georgia, it is illegal
to slap a man on the back or front.

. . . .

Chapter 18 - Medicine

RULE No.908

In Brookfield, Wisconsin, tattooing is illegal unless it is done for medical purposes.

. . . .

RULE No.890

In Trout Creek, Utah, pharmacists may not sell gunpowder to cure headaches.

. . . .

RULE No.109

Citizens may not publicly remove bandages, in Canada.

. . . .

RULE No.777

In Freeport, Maine, mercury thermometers may not be sold, in the city.

. . . .

RULE No.460

In Iceland, anybody is allowed to practice medicine provided they display the word "*Scottulaejnir*" on their door. This loosely translates as 'Quack Doctor'.

. . . .

RULE No.272

In the state of Indiana, you can get out of paying for a dependent's medical care by praying for him/her.

. . . .

Chapter 19 - Merchandise

RULE No.708

In Kentucky, one may not dye a
duckling blue and offer it for sale,
unless more than six are for sale at
once.

. . . .

RULE No.901

In Bellingham, Washington, single-
use, plastic carry out bags are
prohibited.

. . . .

RULE No.899

In the state of Washington, you
cannot buy a mattress on Sundays.

. . . .

RULE No.33

In Bergen County, New Jersey, you
cannot sell clothing, shoes,
furniture, home supplies or
appliances on Sundays.

. . . .

RULE No.873

Hollow logs may not be sold, in the
state of Tennessee.

. . . .

RULE No.879

In the state of Texas, it is illegal to
sell one's eye.

. . . .

RULE No.340

In New Jersey, if you practice
witchcraft or sorcery in order to
trace lost or stolen goods, you can
be taken to court and found guilty
of a misdemeanor.

RULE No.54

In the United Kingdom, you must also purchase a license if you want to purchase a television.

. . . .

RULE No.65

The government of Finland collects a candy tax for goods containing sugar. Cookies do not get taxed, but bottled water does.

. . . .

RULE No.69

In South Africa, you must have a license in order to buy a TV.

. . . .

RULE No.169

In the state of Delaware, it is illegal to sell, barter, or offer the fur of a domestic cat or dog.

. . . .

RULE No.833

In Akron, Ohio, it is illegal to
display colored chickens for sale.

. . . .

RULE No.103

It is illegal to buy and/or sell
nonprescription contacts at
costume shops, in Calgary, Alberta.

. . . .

RULE No.107

You may not pay for a fifty-cent
item with only pennies, in Canada.

. . . .

RULE No.790

In Detroit, Michgan, willfully
destroying your old radio is
prohibited.

. . . .

RULE No.450

In France, the sale of dolls with
alien faces is banned. All dolls must
have human faces.

. . . .

RULE No.747

It is illegal to sell peanuts in Lee
County, Alabama after sundown on
Wednesday.

. . . .

RULE No.509

In Los Angeles, CA, it is illegal for a
customer at a meat market to poke
a turkey, to see how tender it is.

. . . .

RULE No.186

In the state of Pennsylvania, you
cannot barter (swap goods or
services) for a baby.

. . . .

RULE No.354

In Columbus, Ohio, it is against the law for shops to sell corn flakes on Sunday.

. . . .

RULE No.370

In Providence, Pennsylvania it is forbidden to sell toothpaste and a toothbrush to the same customer on a Sunday.

. . . .

RULE No.585

In the state of North Carolina, it is still illegal for people to buy and sell labelled milk crates as they were often used as items of furniture.

. . . .

Chapter 20 - Money

RULE No.334

In the state of New Hampshire, it is illegal to sell the clothes you are wearing to pay off a gambling debt.

. . . .

RULE No.740

In Thailand, it is illegal to step on money.

. . . .

RULE No.238

In the state of Delaware, it is illegal to pawn your wooden leg.

. . . .

RULE No.680

In the state of Hawaii, it is against the law for you to insert coins in your ear.

. . . .

RULE No.632

In Canada, it is illegal to pay with too much change.

. . . .

RULE No.619

It is illegal to flip a coin in a restaurant in Richmond, Virginia, to determine who pays for a meal, as this is considered a form of gambling.

. . . .

RULE No.269

In the state of Indiana, check forgery is punishable with a public flogging of up to 100 lashes.

. . . .

Chapter 21 - Music

RULE No.706

In Topeka, Kanasa, it is illegal to sing the alphabet on the streets at night.

. . . .

RULE No.613

In Salt Lake City, Utah, it is unlawful to carry an unwrapped ukulele in the street.

. . . .

RULE No.241

In Sarasota, Delaware, it is illegal to sing while you are wearing a swimsuit.

. . . .

RULE No.630

It's illegal to whistle in Petrolia,
Ontario.

. . . .

RULE No.627

In Tryon, North Carolina, it is
illegal for anyone to keep fowl that
cackle or for anyone to play the
piccolo between the hours of 11pm
and 7:30am.

. . . .

Chapter 22 - Parking

RULE No.3

In the state of Florida, if an elephant, goat or alligator is left tied to a parking meter, the parking fee has to be paid, just as it would if it were a vehicle.

. . . .

RULE No.854

In Portland, Oregon, trucks may not be parked on the street.

. . . .

RULE No.95

In Denmark, headlights must be on whenever a vehicle is being operated in order to distinguish it from parked cars.

. . . .

RULE No.717

In South Berwick, Maine, it is illegal to park in front of Dunkin Donuts.

. . . .

RULE No.694

In the state of Indiana, you may not back into a parking spot. Police officers cannot see your license plate.

. . . .

Chapter 23 - Politics

RULE No.9

In the state of Arkansas,you are
only allowed 5 minutes to vote.

. . . .

RULE No.397

Virginia State law prohibits
"Corrupt practices of bribery by
any person other than candidates".

. . . .

RULE No.48

In the state of Tennessee, you
must believe in God to be elected
into office.

. . . .

RULE No.822

Idiots may not vote, in the state of
New Mexico.

. . . .

RULE No.451

In France, a law was passed
making it illegal for anyone to stare
at the mayor of Paris.

. . . .

RULE No.745

In the United States, it is a federal
crime to injure a government-
owned lamp.

. . . .

RULE No.516

It is a crime for a teacher or
professor to fail grading the son or
daughter of a fireman in Glenwood
County, Colorado.

. . . .

RULE No.594

In the state of Oklahoma, laughing
at a joke made by a lawyer, is
illegal.

. . . .

RULE No.687

In the state of Illinois, it is legal to
protest naked in front of city hall
as long as you are under 17 years
of age and have legal permits.

. . . .

RULE No.421

In the U.K., placing a postage
stamp that bears the monarch
upside down is considered treason.

. . . .

Chapter 24 - Real Estate

RULE No.912

In the state of Wyoming, all new buildings that cost over $100,000 to build must have 1% of funds spent on art work for the building.

. . . .

RULE No.914

In Wyoming, any person who fails to close a fence is subject to a fine of up to $750.

. . . .

RULE No.29

In Shakopee, Minnesota, it is illegal to bulldoze your house if 5 or more cats are using the ventilation system as their home.

. . . .

RULE No.840

In Clinton, Oklahoma, any person
who leans against a public building
will be subject to fines.

. . . .

RULE No.97

In Denmark, any carport added to
a building increases the value of
the building by 15%.

. . . .

RULE No.317

In the town of Jackson, Mississippi,
if you want to burn your house
down, you must first remove the
roof.

. . . .

RULE No.110

All exterior painting jobs require a
permit (for color), in Canada.

. . . .

RULE No.111

If you have a water trough in your front yard it must be filled by 5:00 am, in Canada.

. . . .

RULE No.112

It is considered an offense to have more than two materials on the outside of one's house, in Canada.

. . . .

RULE No.217

It is against the law for the Arkansas River to rise higher than the Main Street bridge, in Little Rock, Arkansas.

. . . .

RULE No.781

Thistles may not grow in one's yard, in the state of Maryland.

. . . .

RULE No.782

In Rockville, Maryland, it is illegal
to remove a public building by
writing on it.

. . . .

RULE No.794

In Columbia, Missouri, you cannot
have an antenna exposed outside
of your house but you can have a
25-ft satellite dish.

. . . .

RULE No.295

If you are a tenant in Rumford,
Maine, it is illegal for you to bite
your landlord.

. . . .

RULE No.461

In Iceland, anyone caught
trespassing can be fined 1/400th of
a dollar.

. . . .

RULE No.149

In Sweden, you may only own ½
meter down in the ground of any
land you own.

. . . .

RULE No.150

In Sweden, it is illegal to repaint a
house without a painting license
and the government's permission.

. . . .

RULE No.577

In some towns in New Jersey,
garage sales are banned unless the
house is up for sale.

. . . .

RULE No.737

In Helena, Montana, it is illegal to
annoy passersby on sidewalks with
a revolving water sprinkler.

. . . .

RULE No.725

In the state of Minnesota, it is illegal to stand around any building without a good reason to be there.

. . . .

RULE No.733

Exterior burglar bars, which are viewable from the street are not allowed in Ridgeland, Mississippi.

. . . .

RULE No.438

In the Province of Cautin, Chile, it is illegal for any home or public building to exhibit *Playboy* centerfolds and other such material.

. . . .

RULE No.655

Boulders may not be rolled on city property, in Boulder, Colorado.

. . . .

RULE No.628

Certain cities in the United States have designated themselves as 'Stress Free Zones'. Stress is illegal. Anybody seen under stress in these places must be given a free ice cream bar.

. . . .

RULE No.588

South Carolina state law forbids crawling around in public sewers without a permit.

. . . .

RULE No.584

In New York, jaywalking is legal, as long as it's not diagonal. You can cross a street at right angles to the

sidewalk, but you cannot cross it
diagonally.

. . . .

RULE No.415

The city of Guelph, Canada is
classified as a no-pee zone.

. . . .

RULE No.374

In the state of South Dakota, it is
illegal to lie down and fall asleep in
a cheese factory.

. . . .

RULE No.366

In Portland, Oregon, it is against
the law to parade up and down the
street with a 'For Sale' sign.

. . . .

RULE No.358

It is against the law to wash
clothing in a public drinking
fountain or birdbath in Duncan,
Oklahoma.

. . . .

RULE No.620

It is illegal to sleep in an outhouse without the owner's permission, in the state of Washington.

. . . .

Chapter 25 - Religion

RULE No.392

In the state of Vermont, it is unlawful to deny the existence of God.

. . . .

RULE No.396

In Virginia, it is illegal to handle snakes in church.

. . . .

RULE No.328

If your child burps during a church service you may be arrested, in Omaha, Nebraska.

. . . .

RULE No.857

In Pennsylvania, ministers are forbidden from performing marriages when either the bride or groom is drunk.

. . . .

RULE No.218

In the state of California, all animals are banned from mating in public within 1,500 feet of a bar, school, or place of worship.

. . . .

RULE No.456

In Somerset, UK, it was once ordained that people were not to wear the same clothes on Sunday as they did during the rest of the week.

. . . .

RULE No.738

In the Phillippines, divorce is
illegal.

. . . .

RULE No.739

In the Vatican, divorce is illegal.

. . . .

RULE No.440

In Chile, divorce does not exist. Wealthy couples wishing to separate may have the marriage dissolved through a process with a sympathetic judge, in which the couple can claim that their address does not match the one on the marriage certificate.

. . . .

RULE No.204

In the state of Arizona, first cousins cannot marry, unless they are over 65.

. . . .

RULE No.252

In Georgia, it is considered a misdemeanor for anyone to attend

church on Sundays without a
loaded rifle.

. . . .

RULE No.714

Rituals that involve the ingestion of blood, urine, or fecal matter are not allowed, in the state of Louisiana.

. . . .

RULE No.668

One may not whisper in church, in the state of Delaware.

. . . .

RULE No.638

Incestuous marriages are legal, in the state of Alabama.

. . . .

RULE No.363

In the town of Marion, Oregon, ministers are forbidden from eating garlic or onions before delivering a sermon.

. . . .

RULE No.372

Every citizen is obliged to carry his
gun to church, in the state of
South Carolina.

. . . .

RULE No.407

In Nicholas County, West Virginia,
clergy members may not tell jokes
or humorous stories from the
pulpit, during church services.

. . . .

Chapter 26 - Safety

RULE No.902

In Spokane, Washington, persons may not wear a life jacket near the Spokane River.

. . . .

RULE No.817

In the state of New Jersey, one must yield a phone line to a person if it is an emergency.

. . . .

RULE No.129

In Mexico, boneshakers, safety bicycles, and any other similar machines are banned from the center of town.

. . . .

RULE No.291

In New Orleans, Louisiana, fire trucks are required by law to stop at all red lights.

. . . .

RULE No.683

In the state of Idaho, bicycles are not allowed in tennis courts.

. . . .

RULE No.663

In Waterbury, Connecticut, it is illegal for any beautician to hum, whistle, or sing while working on a customer.

. . . .

RULE No.659

In the state of Connecticut, it is illegal to dispose of used razor blades.

. . . .

RULE No.359

In Forgan, Oklahoma, it is illegal to ride your bicycle backwards on the main streets.

. . . .

RULE No.356

In Youngstown, Ohio, it is against the law to ride on the roof of a taxi.

. . . .

Chapter 27 - Sex

RULE No.906

In the state of West Virginia, it is
legal for a male to have sex with
an animal, as long as it does not
exceed 40 lbs.

. . . .

RULE No.539

In Coeur d'Alene, Idaho, any police
officer who suspects that sex is
taking place somewhere must
always drive up from behind, honk
their horn 3 times, and then wait
two minutes before getting out of
their vehicle to investigate.

. . . .

RULE No.30

In the state of Mississippi, it is illegal to seduce a woman if you have no intention of marrying her.

. . . .

RULE No.398

In Lebanon, Virginia, it is against the law to kick your wife out of bed.

. . . .

RULE No.876

In Dyersburg, Tennessee, it is illegal for a woman to call a man for a date.

. . . .

RULE No.880

In Dallas, Texas, it's illegal to possess realistic dildos.

. . . .

RULE No.884

In San Antonio, Texas, it is illegal for both sexes to flirt or respond to flirtation using the eyes and/or hands.

. . . .

RULE No.41

In Toledo, Ohio, it is illegal to hold a piece of cheese in your hand, while talking to the opposite sex.

. . . .

RULE No.46

In the state of Pennsylvania, it is illegal for 16 women to live together in the same house (constitutes a brothel).

. . . .

RULE No.485

In the city of Doha, Qatar, if a man surprises a naked Muslim woman while bathing or dressing she must first cover her face, not her body.

. . . .

RULE No.491

In Saudi Arabia, under no circumstances can any contraception be brought into the country. Anyone caught smuggling birth control pills, condoms, or other contraceptive devices can expect to receive a 6-month prison sentence.

. . . .

RULE No.546

In the state of Illinois, all bachelors must be called master, not mister when addressed by women.

. . . .

RULE No.843

In Schulter, Oklahoma, women may not gamble in the nude, in lingerie, or while wearing a towel.

. . . .

RULE No.821

In the state of New Mexico, nudity
is allowed, provided that male
genitals are covered.

. . . .

RULE No.835

In Oklahoma, it is illegal for the
owner of a bar to allow anyone
inside to pretend to have sex with
a buffalo.

. . . .

RULE No.316

It is against the law to teach others
what polygamy is, in the state of
Mississippi.

. . . .

RULE No.318

Before marriage, a would-be
groom in Truro, Mississippi must
first 'prove himself manly' by

hunting and killing either 6
blackbirds or 3 crows.

. . . .

RULE No.803

Four women may not rent an apartment together, in the suburb of University City, Missouri.

. . . .

RULE No.231

In Pacific Grove, California, you can be fined $500 for 'molesting' butterflies.

. . . .

RULE No.232

In Logan County, Colorado, it is unlawful for a man to kiss a woman while she is asleep.

. . . .

RULE No.124

In Australia, the legal age for straight sex is 16, unless the person is in the care/custody of an older person, in which case it is 18.

. . . .

RULE No.128

In Japan, there is no age of
consent.

. . . .

RULE No.300

It is against the law in Halethorpe,
Maryland to kiss for more than one
second.

. . . .

RULE No.308

In Detroit, Michigan, you can only
make love in a car if it is parked on
your property.

. . . .

RULE No.132

In Mexico, any kind of nude artistic
display, is illegal.

. . . .

RULE No.135

In Norway, prostitution is illegal but being a prostitute is not.

. . . .

RULE No.142

In Singapore, oral sex is illegal unless it is used as a form of foreplay.

. . . .

RULE No.143

In Singapore, as it is considered pornographic, you may not walk around your home nude.

. . . .

RULE No.462

Long ago, in India, a fiancé was required to deflower his future bride if she died before the wedding. She could not be cremated until this ritual was

carried out in front of the village
priest.

. . . .

RULE No.748

In Auburn , Alabama, men who
deflower virgins, regardless of age
or marital status, may face up to 5
years in jail.

. . . .

RULE No.148

While prostitution is legal in
Sweden, it is illegal to use the
services of a prostitute.

. . . .

RULE No.564

In Clawson, Michigan, a farmer can
legally sleep with his pigs, cows,
horses, goats and chickens.

. . . .

RULE No.176

In Michigan, adultery is a felony
punishable by up to 4 years in
prison and a $5,000 fine.

. . . .

RULE No.180

In the state of Nebraska, it is
illegal to marry if you have a
venereal disease.

. . . .

RULE No.524

In Delaware, every minor used to
have to inform his or her parents
before engaging in sexual
intercourse.

. . . .

RULE No.726

In the state of Minnesota, it is
illegal to sleep naked.

. . . .

RULE No.727

In Alexandria, Minnesota, a man is
not allowed to make love to his
wife with the smell of garlic,
onions, or sardines on his breath.

RULE No.188

In Virgina, the state of lovers, sex
is banned, except for married
couples.

. . . .

RULE No.598

In Willowdale, Oregon, men can be
fined for using profane language
during intercourse with their wives.
Their wives can say whatever they
like.

. . . .

RULE No.599

In Harrisburg, Pennsylvania, it is
illegal to have sex with a truck
driver in a tollbooth.

. . . .

RULE No.612

In the state of Texas, men over 50 years old, and one-eyed men are exempt from peeping tom charges.

. . . .

RULE No.716

In Portland, Maine, it's illegal to tickle a girl under the chin with a feather duster.

. . . .

RULE No.722

In Massachusetts, a woman cannot be on top, in sexual activities.

. . . .

RULE No.199

In the state of Maryland, condoms can only be sold in bars.

. . . .

RULE No.195

In North Carolina, a marriage can be declared void if either of the two persons is physically impotent.

. . . .

RULE No.439

It is illegal in Valparaiso, Chile, for a man to take a woman who has committed adultery for his bride.

. . . .

RULE No.441

In China, a law existed which banned any man from looking at the naked feet of another man's wife.

. . . .

RULE No.443

In Beijing, China, it is illegal for a foreigner to take a Chinese woman to his hotel room for sex.

. . . .

RULE No.444

In Ecuador, a young bride can be returned to her parents if her husband discovers she is not a virgin on their wedding night.

. . . .

RULE No.464

Because it is believed that carrot seeds have contraceptive qualities, women in the Indian state of Rajastan are encouraged to eat them.

. . . .

RULE No.465

The law in Iran suggests that sex play between men and wild animals is not recommended, especially when it involves a lioness.

. . . .

RULE No.484

In Russia, the police were once allowed to beat peeping toms soundly.

. . . .

RULE No.485

In Qatar, all forms contraception are strictly forbidden because Qatar needs more males to work

and more females to bear and
raise children.

. . . .

RULE No.692

In the state of Indiana, it is illegal
for a man to be sexually aroused,
in public.

. . . .

RULE No.697

In Indiana, a man over the age of
18 may be arrested for statutory
rape, if the passenger in his car is
not wearing socks and shoes, and
is under the age of 17.

. . . .

RULE No.245

Having sexual relations with a
porcupine is not legal, in the state
of Florida.

. . . .

RULE No.248

In Florida, when having sex, only
the missionary position is legal.

. . . .

RULE No.251

You may not kiss your wife's
breasts, in the state of Florida.

. . . .

RULE No.254

In Idaho, boxes of candy given as
romantic gifts must weigh more
than 50 pounds.

. . . .

RULE No.678

In the state of Georgia, all sex toys
are banned.

. . . .

RULE No.647

In Los Angeles, California, a man is
legally entitled to beat his wife with
a leather belt or strap. However,
the belt cannot be wider than 2
inches...unless he has his wife's
consent to beat her with a wider
strap.

. . . .

RULE No.643

In the state of Arizona, you may not have more than two dildos in a house.

. . . .

RULE No.665

It is illegal for a man to kiss his wife on Sunday in Hartford, Connecticut.

. . . .

RULE No.389

In the state of Utah, you cannot have sex in the back of an ambulance, if it is responding to an emergency call.

. . . .

RULE No.390

Daylight must be visible between partners on a dance floor in Monroe, Utah.

. . . .

RULE No.422

It is illegal in Liverpool, UK for a woman to be topless in public, except as a clerk in a tropical fish store.

. . . .

RULE No.430

In Santa Cruz, Bolivia, it is illegal for a man to have sex with a woman and her daughter, at the same time.

. . . .

RULE No.431

In Santa Cruz, Bolivia, although a woman can legally be a prostitute, it is illegal for her to solicit customers on the street or in any public place.

. . . .

RULE No.432

In Bolivia, women are legally prohibited from drinking more than one glass of wine in bars and restaurants because it is thought to weaken them sexually and makes them easy prey for male advances. Any woman who breaks the law can expect a hefty fine. It is also seen as grounds for divorce.

. . . .

RULE No.433

In the Tupie tribe, in Brazil, a woman must be faithful to her husband; however, he is allowed as many mistresses as he can afford.

. . . .

RULE No.502

In the state of California, cats and dogs have to be licensed before having sex.

. . . .

RULE No.503

In Riverside, California, it is illegal
to kiss unless both people have
wiped their lips with rose water.

. . . .

RULE No.587

Massage parlors are banned in
Hornytown, North Carolina.

. . . .

RULE No.591

In Oxford, Ohio, it is illegal for a
woman to strip in front of a man's
picture.

. . . .

RULE No.618

A man in Norfolk, Virginia can face
up to 60 days in jail for patting a
woman's bottom.

. . . .

RULE No.623

In Romboch, West Virginia, it is
illegal to engage in sexual activity
with the lights on.

. . . .

RULE No.625

In Newcastle, Wyoming, couples
are banned from having sex while
standing inside a store's walk-in
meat freezer.

. . . .

RULE No.533

It is illegal to be caught swimming
in the nude anywhere in the
vicinity of Georgetown, Georgia.
Offenders are transported to the
outskirts of town and left to fend
for themselves. If they partake in
sexual activity whilst skinny
dipping, they are covered with
paint, attached to an ass and
transported out of the town where
they are left and told never to
return.

. . . .

Chapter 28 - Transportation

RULE No.707

In the state of Kansas, if two trains meet on the same track, neither shall proceed until the other has passed.

. . . .

RULE No.4

In Montana, it is illegal to have sheep in the cab of your truck without a chaperone.

. . . .

RULE No.5

In the state of Oregon, a door on a car may not be left open longer than necessary.

. . . .

RULE No.266

In Macomb, Illinois, it is unlawful for a car to impersonate a wolf.

. . . .

RULE No.15

In Walnut, California, it is illegal for a person to fly above an altitude of 10 feet above the ground, or near any electrical conductive public utility wires.

. . . .

RULE No.538

In the town of Idaho Falls, Idaho, anyone over 88 years old is forbidden to ride a motorcycle.

. . . .

RULE No.904

In Wilbur, Washington, you may not ride an ugly horse.

. . . .

RULE No.473

In Italy, it is illegal to take
photographs out of airport
windows.

. . . .

RULE No.31

In Jackson, Mississippi, it is illegal
to have wire cutters in the glove
box of your car.

. . . .

RULE No.400

Only babies are allowed to ride in
baby carriages in Roderfield,
Virginia.

. . . .

RULE No.402

In the state of Washington, a
driver of a car not equipped with
ashtrays is liable to a fine of $200.

. . . .

RULE No.405

In the state of West Virginia, it is against the law to snooze on a train.

. . . .

RULE No.877

In Fayette County, Tennessee, you may not have more than 5 inoperable vehicles on a piece of property.

. . . .

RULE No.881

In Galveston, Texas, no person shall throw trash from an airplane.

. . . .

RULE No.841

In Clinton, Oklahoma, molesting an automobile is illegal.

. . . .

RULE No.83

It is illegal to kiss on railways in France.

. . . .

RULE No.209

In the state of Alaska, it is against the law to look at a moose from an airplane.

. . . .

RULE No.210

It is also unlawful to push a live moose out of a moving airplane, in the state of Alaska.

. . . .

RULE No.789

In the state of Michigan, persons may not be drunk on trains.

. . . .

RULE No.123

In Australia, taxi cabs are required
to carry a bale of hay in the trunk.

. . . .

RULE No.765

In Georgia, you cannot live on a
boat for more than 30 days during
the calendar year, even if you're
just passing through the state.

. . . .

RULE No.457

In Upton, UK, it is illegal for
married couples to live in a
discarded bus.

. . . .

RULE No.581

In New York, it's illegal to use
more than one seat on the subway.

. . . .

RULE No.179

In the state of Montana, steering sheep onto railroad tracks, with the intent of hurting the train (not the sheep) can cost you a fine of $50,000 and up to 5 years in jail.

. . . .

RULE No.525

In Florida, it is illegal to put livestock on board a school bus.

. . . .

RULE No.718

In the state of Maine, you may not step out of a plane while it is in flight.

. . . .

RULE No.202

In Canada, it is illegal to board a plane while it is in flight.

. . . .

RULE No.255

In the town of Pocatello, Idaho, it is prohibited for pedestrians and motorists to display frowns, grimaces, scowls, threatening and glowering looks, gloomy and depressed facial appearances, generally all of which reflect unfavorably upon the city's reputation.

. . . .

RULE No.371

In Central Falls, Rhode Island, it's illegal to pour pickle juice on car tracks.

. . . .

RULE No.373

In Anderson, South Carolina, it is against the law for anyone to curl up on the railway lines and take a nap.

. . . .

RULE No.425

In Bermuda, only one car is
allowed per household.

. . . .

RULE No.426

In Bermuda, you may have as
many motorbikes as you wish, as
long as the engine size is no bigger
than 150cc.

. . . .

RULE No.529

It is illegal for a train to pass
through Gainesville, Florida at a
faster speed than a man can walk.

. . . .

RULE No.681

Residents in the state of Hawaii,
may be fined as a result of not
owning a boat.

. . . .

Chapter 29 - Travel

RULE No.335

In the state of New Hampshire, it is
forbidden to check into a hotel
under an assumed name.

. . . .

RULE No.442

In China, women are prohibited
from walking around a hotel room
naked.

. . . .

RULE No.239

In the state of Delaware, it is
unlawful to fly over any body of
water, unless you are carrying
ample supplies of food and drink
with you.

. . . .

RULE No.586

In North Carolina, all couples staying overnight in a hotel must have a room with double beds with a distance of at least 2 feet between them. Making love in the space between the beds, is not allowed.

. . . .

RULE No.428

In Bermuda, you cannot take a suitcase on a public bus.

. . . .

RULE No.646

Under California state law, it is illegal to peel an orange in a hotel room.

. . . .

Chapter 30 - Weather

RULE No.8

In the United States, it is illegal to issue a fake or counterfeit weather forecast.

. . . .

RULE No.16

It is illegal to collect rainwater in Utah.

. . . .

RULE No.168

In the state of Colorado, you must obtain a permit to modify the weather.

. . . .

RULE No.608

It is a felony in Harrity, Tennessee,
to carry a concealed rain gauge
without permission.

. . . .

*Hope you had a belly laugh (or
two). Thank you for reading!*

The End.

Made in the USA
Middletown, DE
09 December 2023

45170607R00203